Books are to be returned on or before
the last date below.

**Glamorgan Centre for
Art & Design Technology**

Glyntaff Rd, Glyntaff,
Pontypridd CF37 4AT
Tel: 01443 662800

First published in the United States of America
in 2003
by UNIVERSE PUBLISHING,
A Division of Rizzoli International
Publications, Inc.
300 Park Avenue South
New York, NY 10010
www.rizzoliusa.com

2002 2003 2004 2005 2006/10 9 8 7 6 5 4 3 2 1

Printed in Belgium

ISBN: 0-7893-08428

Library of Congress Catalog Control Number:
2002115764

NOT TEFLON: MTV DESIGN + PROMOS
EDITED BY JEFFREY KEYTON

NOT TEFLON IS ABOUT WHAT   STICKS.

                                        IT ALL STICKS TO SOME DEGREE. CERTAINLY YOUR
VISUAL HISTORY AND YOUR PAST SUCCESSES COME TO MIND; HOWEVER, I JUST CANNOT
SEEM TO ESCAPE THE CREATIVE TITILLATION OF THE MOMENT. EVOLUTION THRIVES AT MTV, A
CREATIVE CULTURE THAT IS CONSTANTLY SEARCHING FOR GREAT IDEAS AND EXPERIMENTA-
TION, BECAUSE GREAT IDEAS WILL ALWAYS STICK AND BE RELEVANT AND FOREVER OUTLIVE
THE TEFLON OF POPULAR CULTURE. STAGNATION EQUALS DEATH, SO WE CREATE, WE THRIVE,
WE STAY ALIVE. WE BOUNCE, WE ROCK, WE WORK FOR OUR AUDIENCE. IT'S FAST AND FURI-
OUS AND NOT FOR THE FAINT OF HEART, AND, LIKE A GREAT SONG, THE BEAT DRIVES YOU.
JUST LET GO AND EMBRACE THE STRESS TO TOP YOURSELF; LET YOUR MIND RUN FREE.
"EASIER SAID THAN DONE," YOU SAY, BUT CREATIVE CONSTIPATION IS NOT AN OPTION HERE,
SO YOU LEARN TO SURVIVE. IT HELPS THAT THERE IS STRENGTH IN NUMBERS AND EVERYONE
AROUND YOU IS A JUNKIE FOR THE SAME THING AND WILL GIVE YOU A GOOD KICK IN THE ASS
FOR A LAME, REDUNDANT IDEA.

        OH…I'M GETTING OFF THE SUBJECT. *NOT TEFLON* IS ABOUT RECENT WORK—THE IDEAS AND
THE INSPIRATIONS. THIS BOOK FEATURES WORK FROM AN ECLECTIC GROUP OF TALENT UNITED BY
A PASSION FOR MUSIC, ARTISTRY, EXPERIMENTATION, HUMOR, AND THE CHANNEL ITSELF, AND
BOUND BY A COMMITMENT TO DO GREAT WORK FOR AN ORGANIZATION THAT EXPECTS AND SUPPORTS
IT; FOR THAT WE ARE ALL THANKFUL.

        HEY, IT'S LIKE YOU NEVER LEFT ART SCHOOL, NEVER GREW UP, NEVER MATURED…STILL FEEL-
ING THE JOY OF YOUR FIRST CRUSH. HOWEVER, *NOT TEFLON* FEELS VERY GROWN-UP. SELECT
WORK FROZEN IN A BOOK CAN BE SCARY AT TIMES, BUT IT FEELS GOOD TO LOOK BACK AND
CATCH YOUR BREATH FOR A SECOND.

NOW THE MOMENT CALLS FOR ME TO STOP PONTIFICATING AND FOR YOU TO ENJOY THE BOOK.—J.K.

INT

I'M SURE THAT WE'VE ALL HAD THE SAME EXPERIENCE, WATCHING MTV AND BEING NUMBED AND UNDERWHELMED BY THE MILLION DOLLAR VIDEOS AND BEACH-HOUSE PROGRAMMING, BUT BEING CAPTIVATED BY THE GRAPHICS AND VISUALS THAT MTV USES TO INTRODUCE THEIR PROGRAMS.

I'M NOT LOOKING TO MAKE ENEMIES OR BE A COMPLAINER, BUT THERE IS A DEARTH OF CREATIVITY IN THE WORLD OF MUSIC. MARKETING HAS, IN MANY CASES, REPLACED CREATIVITY, AND HOMOGENEITY HAS OFTEN REPLACED IDIOSYNCRASY AND PERSONALITY, WHICH IS WHY MTV'S GRAPHICS STAND OUT IN SUCH SHARP RELIEF TO THE NUMBING AND UNDERWHELMING POP-MUSIC FODDER THAT THEY OFTEN INTRODUCE. IN MANY WAYS, THE GRAPHICS AND VISUALS THAT MTV GENERATE THEMSELVES (AND THAT ARE CONTAINED IN THIS BOOK) ARE THE ON-AIR REPRESENTATION OF THE CHALLENGING AND CONTROVERSIAL SPIRIT THAT ORIGINALLY CHARACTERIZED YOUTH-MUSIC CULTURE. AS POP AND ROCK ACTS HAVE SLOWLY BECOME SAFER AND MORE GENERIC, THE SPIRIT OF CONTROVERSY AND CHARACTER THAT USED TO BE INHERENT IN THE MUSIC ITSELF HAS BEEN ALL BUT THOROUGHLY EXORCISED.

<u>ANOTHER MANUFACTURED AND GENERIC POP ACT? EH, WHO CARES.</u>
<u>ANOTHER MANUFACTURED AND GENERIC MODERN ROCK ACT? EH, WHO CARES.</u>
<u>ANOTHER MANUFACTURED AND GENERIC R&B ACT? EH, WHO CARES.</u>

BUT LOOK AT THOSE AMAZING GRAPHICS. AND LOOK AT THE COOL VISUALS THAT THE CREATIVE PEOPLE AT MTV HAVE COME UP WITH THEMSELVES.

JUST RECENTLY I WAS AT THE 2002 VIDEO MUSIC AWARDS AND I COULDN'T HELP BUT NOTICE THAT THE BEST THING ABOUT THE AWARDS (APART FROM TRIUMPH THE INSULT COMIC DOG) WERE THE VISUALS THAT MTV HAD GENERATED TO INTRODUCE EACH AWARD. THE MUSICIANS THEMSELVES WERE ALL SINCERELY AND HUMBLY BOWING DOWN TO THE ALTAR OF COMMERCE AND MARKETING, LEAVING THE GRAPHICS (AND TRIUMPH) AS THE ONLY ICONOCLASTIC AND IRREVERENT FACETS OF THE WHOLE PRODUCTION.

WHAT IS MOST SATISFYING ABOUT THESE IRREVERENT AND COMPELLING VISUALS IS THAT THEY REACH MILLIONS AND MILLIONS OF PEOPLE. THERE'S A LOT OF CHALLENGING AND GROUNDBREAKING DESIGN WORK BEING DONE IN THE WORLD TODAY, BUT MOST OF IT REMAINS UNSEEN OR UNNOTICED EXCEPT BY A SMALL URBAN COGNOSCENTI. THE CHALLENGING AND COMPELLING GRAPHICS CONTAINED IN THIS BOOK ARE EXTRA-SPECIAL BECAUSE THEY REACH INTO THE HEARTLAND WHERE THEY SERVE AS A SMALL BUT SATISFYING BEACON OF INTEGRITY AND INVENTION. IF YOU LOOK AT THE LIST OF 'THINGS WE DON'T WANT TO BE' PRESENTED IN THE BEGINNING PAGES YOU MIGHT THINK, AS I DID UPON READING IT, THAT GLUEING A COPY OF THIS LIST TO THE FOREHEADS OF THE MAJORITY OF THE PEOPLE INVOLVED IN THE WORLD OF MUSIC MIGHT NOT BE SUCH A BAD IDEA. IN READING THIS LIST, YOU REALIZE THAT IF THE PEOPLE WHO GENERATE THE GRAPHICS AND VISUALS FOR MTV HAVE SET OUT NOT TO BE THESE THINGS (DEFANGED, ANEMIC, HUMDRUM, ETC.), THEN THEY HAVE, THANKFULLY, SUCCEEDED.

ENJOY THE BOOK. MAKE BETTER MUSIC.

THANKS,
MOBY
NYC, SEPTEMBER 2002

THINGS WE DON'T WANT TO BE:

routine. trite. jejune. anemic. safe. humdrum. derivative. indistinct. dull. tasteless. expected.

defanged. average. lifeless. dull. trifling. insipid. staid. prudish. garden-variety. trivial. cautious.

toothless. vapid. shoddy. bourgeois. quaint. bland. timid. standard. slipshod. banal. mediocre.

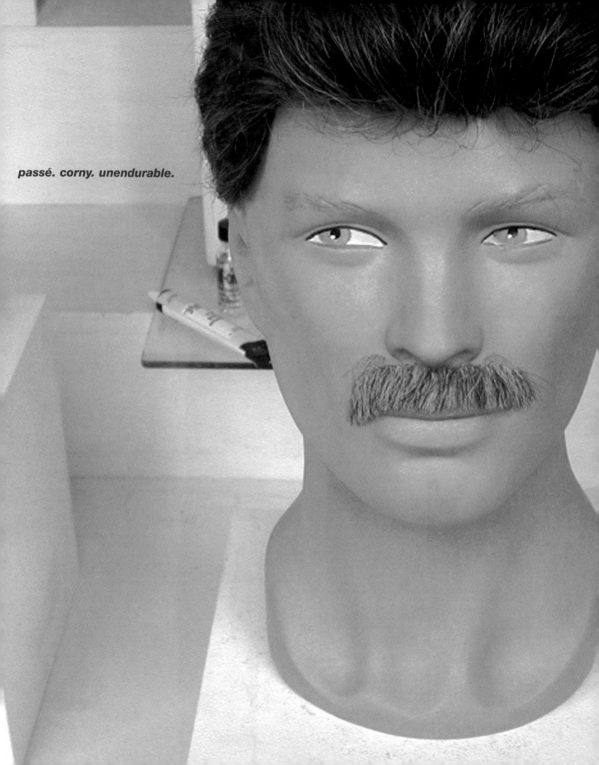

passé. corny. unendurable.

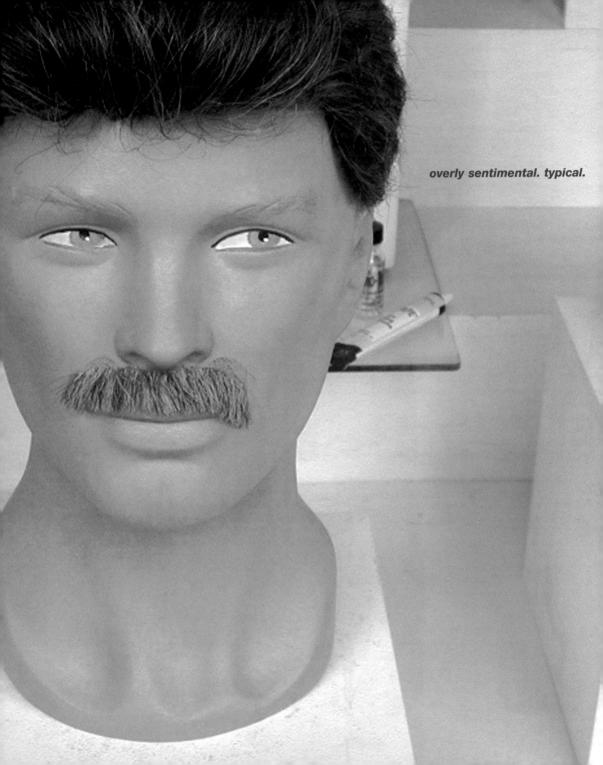

overly sentimental. typical.

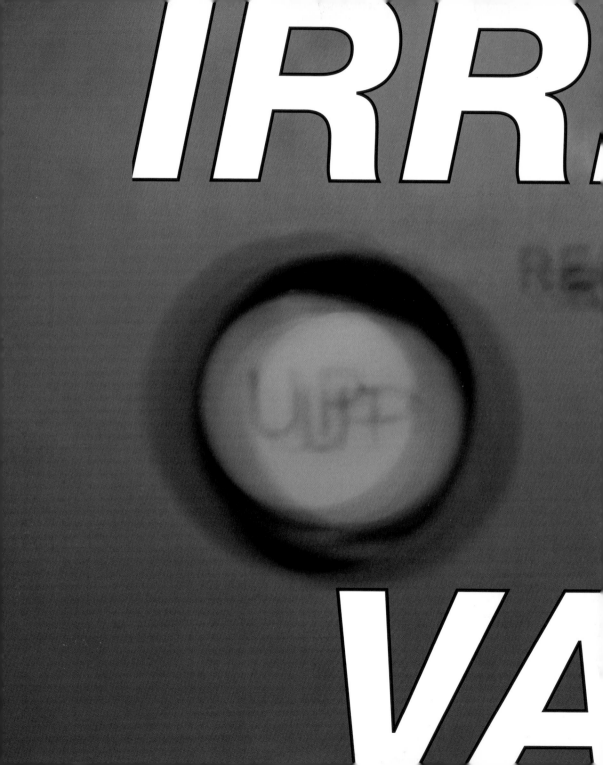

THINGS WE ARE:

TRADITIONALLY, PROGRAM BOOKS FOR AWARDS SHOWS ARE STUFFY DOCUMENTS OF THE VARIOUS CATEGORIES' NOMINATIONS AND A COLLECTION OF ADS. THE VIDEO MUSIC AWARDS ARE THE ANTI-AWARDS SHOW, A VENUE WHERE THE ONLY TRADITION IS RULE BREAKING. WITH THAT IN MIND THE PROGRAM BOOK WORKS TO REINVENT ITSELF EVERY YEAR.

PRINT/ *COMMON* – 2001 VIDEO MUSIC AWARDS BOOK: IT HAD BEEN A WHILE SINCE WE HAD A "PRO-SOCIAL" THEME TO A VMA BOOK. AT THE TIME, MTV WAS RUNNING A "PRO-SOCIAL" CAMPAIGN ABOUT TOLERANCE AND DIVERSITY, SO IT MADE SENSE TO TIE INTO THAT AND BRING IT TO LIFE IN A PRINT FORM. THE QUESTION WAS: HOW. WE REALIZED THAT THERE IS GREAT DIVERSITY IN OUR COMMON EXPERI-ENCES: SLEEP, PAIN, JOY, PARENTS, BREATH, BLISS, PRIDE, SORROW, WORSHIP, HAIR AND LOVE. THIS LIST OF WORDS WAS GIVEN TO THE TALENTED ERIC JOHNSON TO INTERPRET THROUGH PHOTOGRAPHY. WE WANTED A VERY FINE-ART LOOK AND FEEL TO THE DESIGN AND PHOTOGRAPHY. IT WAS BITTERSWEET, HOWEVER, IN ITS UNINTENTIONAL TIMELINESS, FOR THIS BOOK'S DEBUT AT THE SHOW WAS TWO DAYS BEFORE SEPTEMBER 11. AS CHUCK D SO ELO-QUENTLY WROTE IN HIS INTRODUCTION TO THE BOOK, "IN OTHER WORDS, BE ABOVE ALL OTHER ANIMALS, SPECIES AND CREATURES BY LEARNING AND SHARING CULTURE AND REALLY 'DO OUR THING' BY TAKING CARE OF THE ONLY SPOT IN THE UNIVERSE WE KNOW OF."

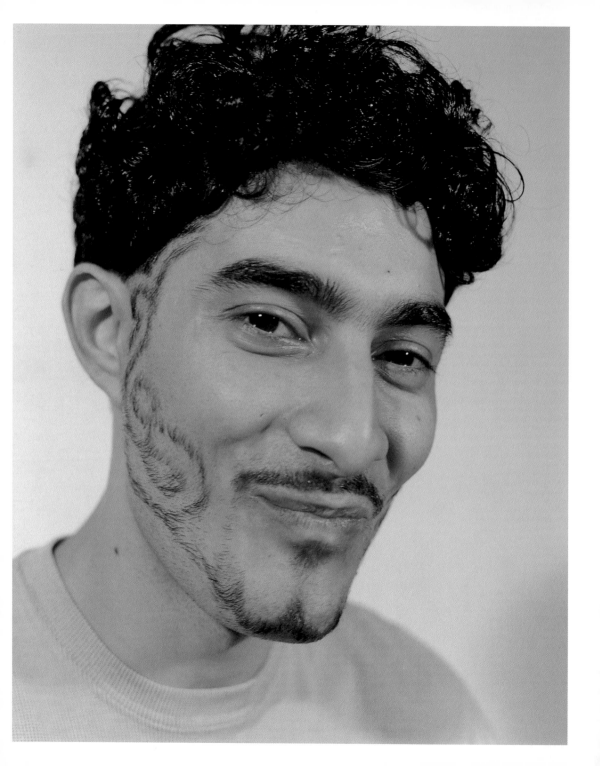

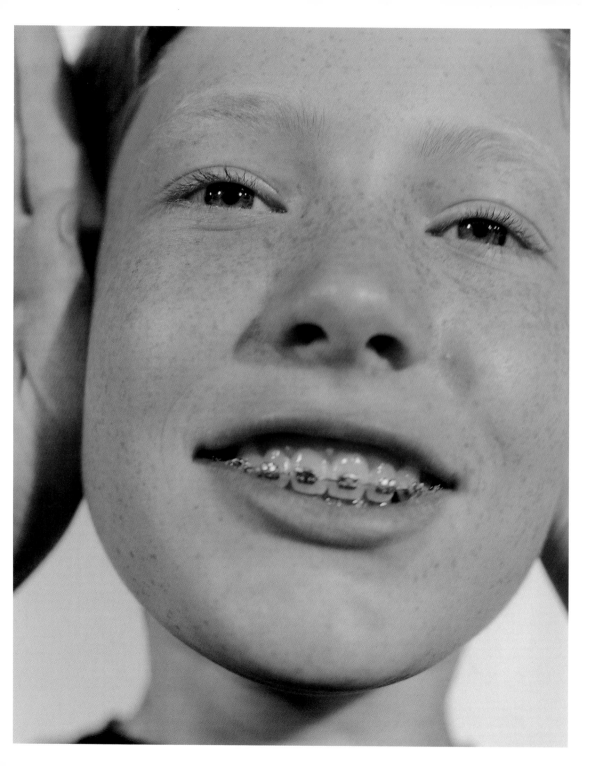

ON-AIR PROMO/ EMOTICON CRYING, 2001: MTV.COM HAD REDONE ITS ENTIRE LOOK, ADDING A LOT OF COMMUNITY-RELATED CAPABILITIES. IN TRYING TO FIND THE MOST COMPELLING VISUALS FROM THE NEW SITE TO TEASE THE RELAUNCH, WE STUMBLED UPON THESE ANIMATED "EMOTICONS" (WHICH WERE USED TO SHOW ATTITUDE ON MTV.COM'S MESSAGE BOARDS). THIS ONE WAS ESPECIALLY COMPELLING, EVEN ODDLY MOVING.   EVERYONE HAS HAD CRYING EXPERIENCES. I USED TO CRY IN THE BATHROOM, WHERE NO ONE COULD SEE ME. THERE I'D EVALUATE THE SITUATIONS THAT CAUSED MY SORROW. I'D ALSO LOOK IN THE MIRROR AND WATCH MY EYES WELL UP. THEN MY BLINKING EYELIDS WOULD MAKE MY TEARS FALL. THIS MOTION WAS MY INSPIRATION FOR THE CRYING-EYE EMOTICON PROMO, CREATED FOR THE RELAUNCH OF MTV.COM. SINCE THE PROMO HAD TO CAPTURE A SPECIFIC EMOTION, THE COMPOSITION WAS KEPT SIMPLE. THE ELEMENTS WERE CREATED IN ILLUSTRATOR. THE ANIMATION WAS RENDERED IN AFTER EFFECTS. THE MUSIC COMPOSER, INSPIRED BY THE VISUALS, CREATED A UNIQUE MUSICAL INTERPRETATION OF CRYING. WITHOUT ANY VOICE-OVER, THE STRONG AND STEADY SOUND OF A STRING ORCHESTRA IN MINOR KEYS (VERSUS THE NORMAL FRENZIED DIN OF TELEVISION COMMERCIALS), PLUS THE MINIMALIST VISUALS, WERE WHAT MADE THE CRYING EYE.

EMOTICONS

EMOTICONS

express yourself now at the new mtv.com

express yourself now at the new mtv.com

express yourself now at the new mtv.com

what connects you?

what connects you?

what connects you?

what connects you?

ON-AIR PROMO/ TRAVELOGUE, A 2002 MTV IMAGE CAMPAIGN: BASICALLY, MTV FOLLOWS YOU WHEREVER YOU GO. PEOPLE OF EARTH...THERE IS NO ESCAPE.

ON-AIR DESIGN/ 2002 VIDEO MUSIC AWARDS NOMINEE PACKAGING:
TO INTRODUCE THE NOMINEES FOR THE 2002 VIDEO MUSIC AWARDS,
WE GOT EXTREMELY IRREVERENT BY MAKING FUN OF OUR OWN
AWARDS STATUE. ACTUAL-SIZE MOON MEN WERE TRANSFORMED
INTO FUNCTIONING APPLIANCES AND INFOMERCIAL PRODUCTS THAT
CONCEPTUALLY SUITED EACH CATEGORY: A SPRINKLER (BEST
DANCE), A SAUSAGE MAKER (BEST MALE), A THIGHMASTER (BEST
R&B) AND A NUTCRACKER (BEST FEMALE) WERE JUST A FEW. WE
THEN SHOT 15-SECOND MINI-INFOMERCIAL STYLE PIECES SHOWING
EACH PRODUCT AND ALL OF ITS AMAZING USES! (CUE STUDIO
APPLAUSE TRACK.) SOME WERE ACCOMPANIED BY COMMERCIAL-
INSPIRED VOICE-OVERS OR JINGLES, WHILE OTHERS WERE SIMPLY
UNDERSCORED BY MUSIC.

AUDIO:
[Polka music accompanies the butcher as he makes the numerous sausage links. At the end of the spot, there is audience applause and approval.]

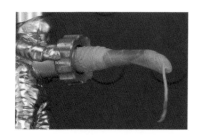

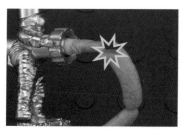
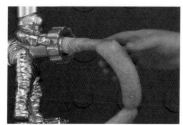
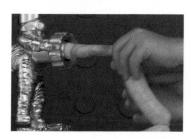

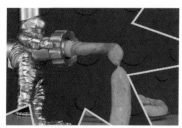
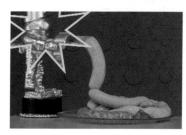

AUDIO:
[The sound of sprinkler turning on. Once the sprinkler has done one-half of a rotation, a disco beat kicks in, accompanying the sound of the sprinkler.]

ON-AIR DESIGN/ 2001 VIDEO MUSIC AWARDS NOMINEE PACKAGING: MTV OFF AIR CREATIVE'S HEAD, JEFFREY KEYTON, CAME UP WITH THE IDEA OF USING NATURE FOOTAGE FOR THE PACKAGING. OPEN TO ALL THINGS THAT WALK, CRAWL, SWIM, AND SLITHER IN THE ANIMAL KINGDOM BUT LACKING SPECIFIC DIRECTION, WE WENT TO THE NATIONAL GEOGRAPHIC HEADQUARTERS TO DIG THROUGH ITS ARCHIVES. WE SPENT DAYS SIFTING THROUGH MOUNTAINS OF NATURE FOOTAGE FOR THINGS THAT MIGHT CONCEPTUALLY FIT EACH VIDEO CATEGORY OR WERE JUST SO BIZARRE YOU COULDN'T LOOK AWAY. AFTER GORGING OURSELVES ON FORNICATING MONKEYS, CANNIBALISTIC SOUTH AMERICAN RODENTS, AND OTHER ODDITIES, WE RETURNED WITH A CLIP REEL OF SELECT FAVORITES. FROM THERE, IT WAS A BACK-AND-FORTH PROCESS OF EDITING THEN WRITING, OF WRITING THEN EDITING, TO MAKE SURE THAT EACH CATEGORY HAD PROPER ANIMAL REPRESENTATION. BUT TO BE HONEST, SOME OF THE BEST "WRITING" HAPPENED IN THE VOICE-OVER SESSION, LIKE DURING THE READING FOR THE BEST POP VIDEO CATEGORY, IN WHICH WE FORCED THE VERY PROPER AND BRITISH PAUL HECHT (THE VOICE-OVER) TO SAY "BOOBIES" IN AS MANY WAYS AS POSSIBLE, JUST BECAUSE IT WAS FUNNY TO HEAR HIM SAY IT. BOOBIES BOOBIES BOOBIES.

AUDIO: "Best Pop. Ah! Look at all those boobies!
If one booby does it, the others follow."

AUDIO: "Best Rap. Hippopotami can consume over 100 pounds of grass a day!"

PRINT/ 2000 VIDEO MUSIC AWARDS PRINT CAMPAIGN: FROM THE OPERA HOUSE TO RADIO CITY MUSIC HALL: THE CREATIVE TEAM TOOK THE DIRECTION OF BEING NYC-CENTRIC THIS TIME AROUND. WE MET FOR LUNCH WITH DAVID LACHAPELLE AT HIS STUDIO. DAVID REALLY JUMPED ON THE DIRECTION, AND WITHIN MINUTES HIS HIGHLY CREATIVE MIND WAS RATTLING OFF IDEAS. DAVID IS ONE OF THE VERY FEW TALENTS THAT I CAN SAY HAS TRUE UNBRIDLED CREATIVITY, AND IT'S VERY CONTAGIOUS. IMMEDI-ATELY WE WERE ALL BOUNCING IDEAS OFF EACH OTHER AND HAVING A GREAT TIME. WE QUICKLY KNEW THAT THIS DIRECTION WOULD HAVE ENOUGH LEGS FOR A CAMPAIGN.

IRONICALLY, DUE TO SCHEDULING CONFLICTS WITH THE ARTISTS, ONLY THE CHILI PEPPERS WERE ACTUALLY SHOT IN NEW YORK CITY.

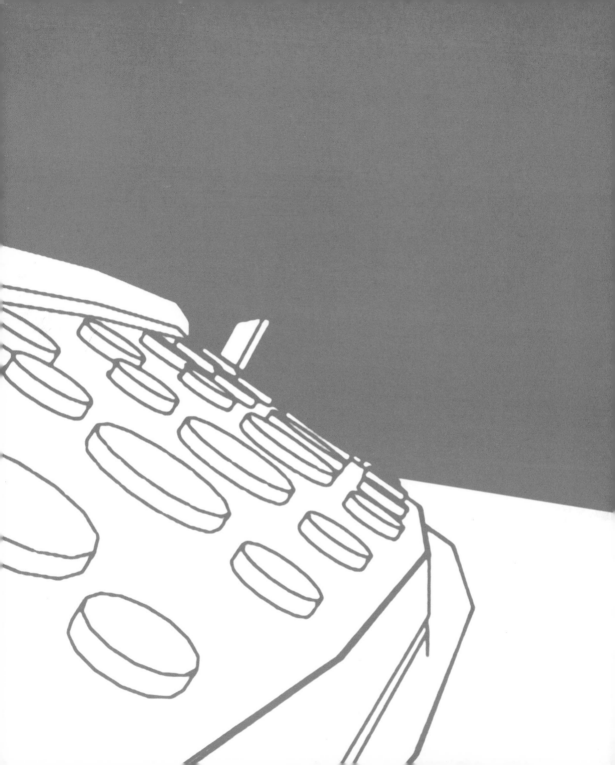

ON-AIR DESIGN/ SPANKIN' NEW MUSIC WEEK, 2001: THIS PIECE IS REALLY AN HOMAGE TO THE BASIC DJ EQUIPMENT: THE TURNTABLE, HEADPHONES, AND MIXER. FOR DECADES THESE MACHINES HAVE HELPED TO EXCITE CULTURE AND YET HAVE ALWAYS REMAINED IRON-ICALLY STATIC, NOT RESPONDING TO THE MOVEMENT AND AGITATION THEY GENERATE. IT DOESN'T MATTER IF YOU PLAY A TECHNO RECORD WITH THE HEAVIEST REPETITIVE BASS OR SOME MELODIC CLASSICAL MUSIC; VISUALLY, THE EXPERIENCE IS IDENTICAL. WE WANTED TO END WITH THE STATIONARY NATURE OF THIS EQUIPMENT AND HAVE IT RESPOND TO THE MUSIC IT GENER-ATES. TO DO THIS, I USED A SPECIAL TYPE OF ANIMATION TECHNIQUE IN WHICH AN AUDIO WAVE IS CONVERTED INTO AN ANIMATION CHANNEL THAT CAN DRIVE MOVEMENT IN THREE-DIMENSIONAL SPACE. HAVING THIS DIRECT RELATIONSHIP BETWEEN SOUND AND MOTION MAKES THE AUDIO THE SINGLE MOST IMPORTANT ELEMENT OF THE PIECE SINCE IT LITERALLY DICTATES ALL OF THE MOVEMENT, RHYTHM, AND PACE OF THE ANIMATION. VISUALLY, I DECIDED TO USE AN OUTLINE RENDERER THAT RECALLS TECHNICAL DIAGRAMS, WHICH HELP TO DESCRIBE WITH PRECI-SION ALL THE MODELED COMPONENTS OF EACH OF THE MACHINES AND ADDS A GRAPHIC FEEL TO THE ANIMATION.

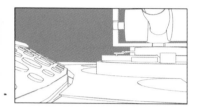 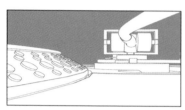 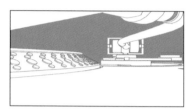

  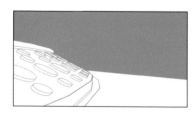

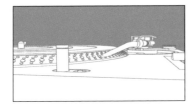

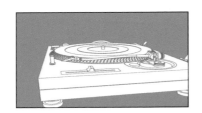

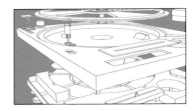

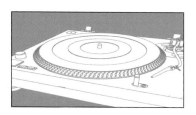 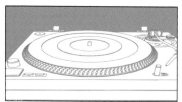 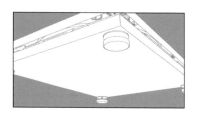

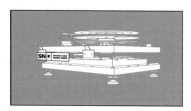 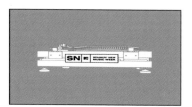 

LOARA HIGH
SCHOOL POOL
1765 WEST
CERRITOS AVENUE
ANAHEIM, CA

GWEN STEFANI
SWIMS FOR HER
HIGH SCHOOL TEAM
HERE IN 1986.

ON-AIR PROMO/ MTV 20 PLACES, 2001: THIS IDEA WAS
INSPIRED BY AN INTERVIEW WITH BREAL FROM CYPRESS
HILL THAT TOOK PLACE AT A RECORDING STUDIO IN THE
SAN FERNANDO VALLEY, CALIFORNIA. THE OUTSIDE OF
THE DECREPIT BUILDING LOOKED LIKE A RUINED
STUCCO STRIP MALL, BUT INSIDE, SOME OF THE MOST
IMPORTANT HIP HOP RECORDS OF THE LAST DECADE
HAD BEEN RECORDED. WE WANTED TO MEMORIALIZE
SOME OF THESE FORGOTTEN OR SEEMINGLY INSIGNIF-
ICANT PLACES WHERE MUSIC HISTORY HAPPENED. WE
VISITED THE LOCATIONS WHERE FAMOUS VIDEOS WERE
SHOT, STUDIOS WHERE ICONIC ALBUMS WERE
RECORDED, AND MANY OF THE HIGH SCHOOLS THAT
VARIOUS MUSIC LUMINARIES ATTENDED.

**205TH STREET PARK
HOLLIS AVENUE
QUEENS, NY**

**RUN DMC
FIRST PRACTICED
AND PERFORMED
HERE IN 1979.**

ON-AIR PROMO/ THE CHICKEN WASHER, 1998: I WISH I COULD TAKE COMPLETE CREDIT FOR THE MADNESS THAT IS THE IMAGE OF A WOMAN WASHING A CHICKEN FOR THE 1998 VIDEO MUSIC AWARDS IMAGE CAMPAIGN. BUT ALAS, THE TRUTH IS, I CAME UP WITH THE IDEA AFTER FINDING A PHOTO FROM THE FIFTIES OF JUST THIS SORT OF THING. I THREW IN THE LAUNDROMAT, A HAIRY GUY WEARING A WIFE-BEATER (NOW THAT'S FUNNY), SOME DIALOGUE ABOUT THE STATE OF MODERN MUSIC, AND A PROMO WAS BORN. WHAT BETTER WAY TO GET THE ATTENTION OF THE MTV AUDIENCE THAN A CAMPAIGN REVOLVING AROUND STRANGE CHARACTERS, IN EVEN STRANGER SITUATIONS, RANTING ABOUT MUSIC?

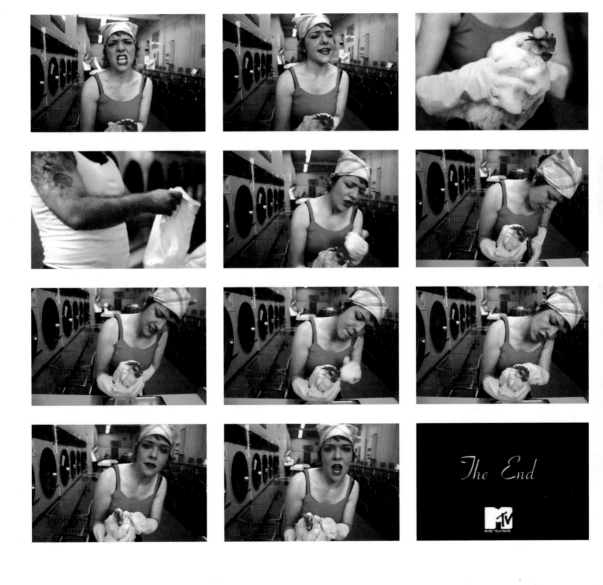

VIDEO MU
AWARDS

hosted by JIMMY FALLON

LIVE NYC

PRINT/ 2002 VIDEO MUSIC AWARDS PRINT CAMPAIGN: SEPTEMBER 11 OBVIOUSLY CHANGED OUR LIVES. THE FOLLOWING YEAR, THE USUAL WEEK THE VMA'S APPEARED WAS CHANGED SO AS TO AVOID ALL THE TELEVISED EVENTS GOING ON AROUND THE FIRST ANNIVERSARY. OUR TASK WAS TO COMMUNICATE THE DATE CHANGE TO OUR AUDIENCE WHILE AT THE SAME TIME NODDING TO THE EVENTS OF SEPTEMBER 11 IN A POSITIVE AND SUBTLE MANNER. WE WANTED TO EXPRESS THAT NEW YORK AND THE DIVERSITY OF ITS PEOPLE IS VERY MUCH ALIVE AND WELL. A SIX-FOOT CUTOUT BLOWUP OF THE MOON MAN WAS MADE AND GIVEN TO DAVID LACHAPELLE TO PHOTO-GRAPH IN A VERY SPIRITED AND DIRECT REPORTAGE STYLE. JIMMY AND THOMAS FROM OFF-AIR CREATIVE RAN AROUND THE CITY GUERRILLA-STYLE WITH DAVID FOR THREE DAYS GRABBING EVERYDAY PEOPLE OFF THE STREETS TO BE IN OUR ADS. IT WAS A HIGHLY EFFECTIVE CAMPAIGN. BETWEEN SEPTEMBER 11 AND THE UNTIMELY DEATH OF HIS LONGTIME STUDIO ASSISTANT, LUIS ENUZ, DAVID HAD PRETTY MUCH ABANDONED NEW YORK. THROUGH THIS ASSIGNMENT, HE AGAIN SAW THE SPIRIT, THE ENERGY, AND THE VITALITY THAT THRIVES IN OUR BELOVED CITY.

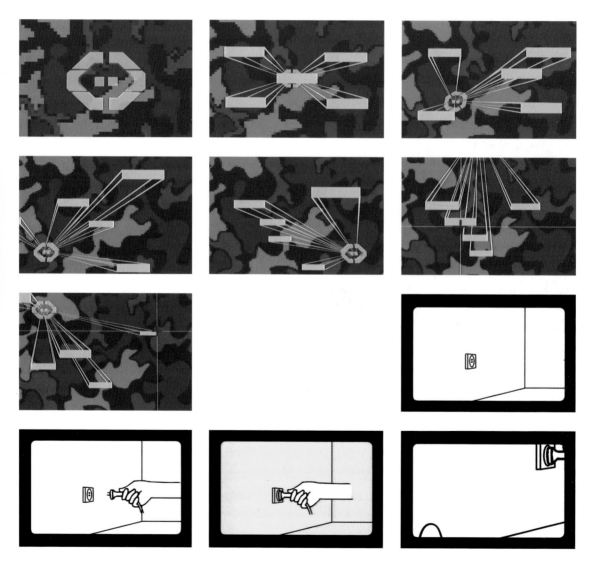

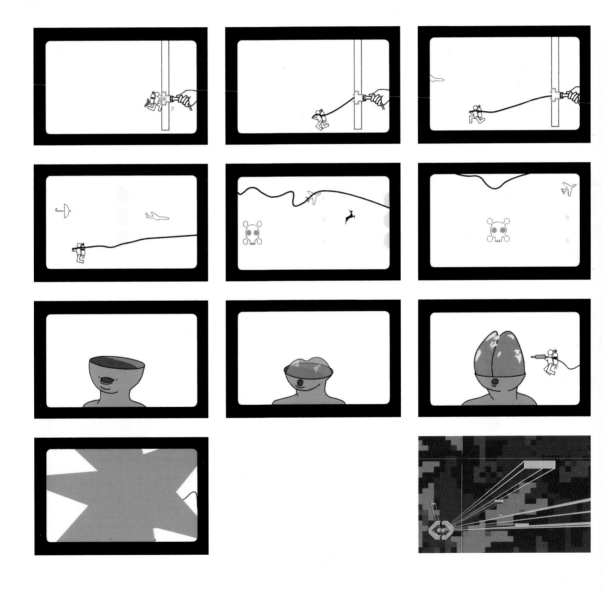

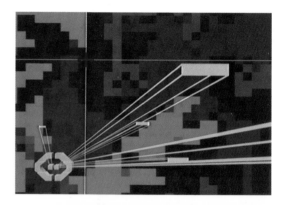

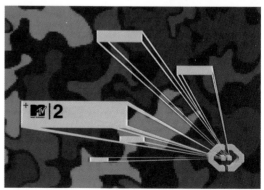

ON-AIR DESIGN/ 2001 MTV2 CHANNEL REDESIGN: MTV2'S LAUNCH TO DIGITAL CABLE WAS AN IMPORTANT ONE. THE CONCEPT WAS A RETURN TO THE GRASSROOTS IDEOLOGY THAT MTV HAD EMBRACED 20 YEARS PRIOR, BY FEATURING A VARIETY OF CUTTING-EDGE ANIMATIONS. WE SEARCHED ALL OVER THE WORLD FOR NEW TALENT AND EITHER FOUND OR COMMISSIONED 10-SECOND SPOTS FROM AROUND THE GLOBE. IN ORDER TO USE THESE SPOTS TO INTRODUCE THE MTV2 PROGRAMMING, A FIVE SECOND BUMP-IN AND A FIVE SECOND BUMP-OUT WAS DESIGNED TO BOOKEND THE UNIQUE SPOTS.

SINCE THE CHANNEL'S POSITIONING WAS ABOUT INTERACTIVITY, A SIMPLE ICON WAS DEVELOPED TO BRAND THE CHANNEL AND SERVE AS A SYMBOL THAT REPRE-SENTED A DIGITAL PORTAL. EXTERNAL GRAPHIC BARS EMANATE FROM THE MAIN ICON TO SERVE AS SEPARATE INTERACTIVE SEGMENTS THAT A VIEWER WOULD CLICK ON TO ACCESS A PARTICULAR REALM OF MTV2 ACTIVITY. A VARIETY OF CAMOUFLAGE PATTERNS MIXED WITH UNUSUAL COLORS SERVED AS A BACKGROUND THAT MORPHED AND PIXELATED.

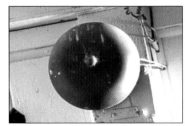

INTERNATIONAL ON-AIR PROMO ASIA/ BRITNEY SPOOF, 1999: I WROTE AND DIRECTED THIS PROMO FOR OUR "I LIKE" TAG LINE CAMPAIGN. I WAS LOOKING FOR SOMETHING TO ILLUSTRATE THE OBSESSION OF SOUTHEAST ASIA'S YOUNG PEOPLE WITH MTV. THE CHALLENGE WAS TO MAKE YOUNG PEOPLE IN FIVE OR SIX COUNTRIES IN THE REGION CONNECT WITH IT, BUT GIVEN OUR BUDGET, WE COULD HARDLY SHOOT FIVE OR SIX DIFFERENT VERSIONS. THE UNIFYING ELEMENT ACROSS THESE COUNTRIES HAD TO BE MUSIC AND MUSIC VIDEOS. MY THOUGHTS IMMEDIATELY WENT TO THE TIMES WHEN I USED TO DAY-DREAM IN CLASS ABOUT BEING DAVE GAHAN OF DEPECHE MODE IN THE VIDEO "PEOPLE ARE PEOPLE." BRITNEY'S "...BABY ONE MORE TIME" WAS THE PREDOMINANT SOUND OF THE MOMENT, AND AS I WAS TRAVELLING AROUND THE REGION, I THOUGHT IT WOULD BE FUNNY TO SEE A YOUNG GIRL IN A RURAL CLASSROOM IMAGINING HERSELF IN THE VIDEO. A DAYDREAM IS SOMETHING EVERYONE CAN RELATE TO. THE CLASSROOM, CLASSMATES, AND STERN TEACHER ARE ALSO UNIVERSAL. WE DECIDED TO SHOOT IN MANILA, SINCE THE SINGING AND DANCING TALENT IN THE CITY IS IMPRESSIVE AND WE COULD FIND YOUNG PEOPLE WITH A FAIRLY GENERIC "SOUTHEAST ASIAN" LOOK. MY PREFERENCE FOR AN IMAGE/PROMO SPOT IS ALWAYS FOR THOSE WITH A STORY LINE AND A SURPRISE, HUMOROUS ENDING AS THE PAYOFF. PERSONALLY, I FEEL THAT A STORY CONNECTS BETTER WITH OUR VIEWERS, STAYS IN THEIR MINDS LONGER, AND HAS THE POTENTIAL TO BECOME A TOPIC OF CONVERSATION WITH THEIR PEERS, LEADING TO MORE AWARENESS OF THE CHANNEL AND, HOPEFULLY, INCREASED VIEWERSHIP.

AUDIO open: "Um...I love it when they blur stuff out
and then expect you to believe...like...
what's behind that? Like, if I go like this
[holds up middle finger] they'll blur it out...
but who doesn't know what I'm doing?"

AUDIO close: "They should blur random stuff
just to throw us off."

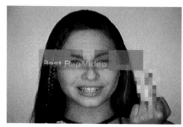

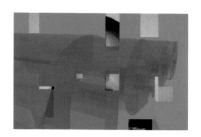

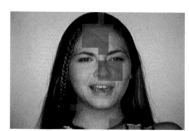

ON-AIR DESIGN/ 2000 VIDEO MUSIC AWARDS NOMINEE
PACKAGING: MTV'S ASPIRATIONAL AUDIENCE WAS PUT IN
THE SPOTLIGHT TO INTRODUCE THE VIDEO NOMINEES FOR
THE 2001 VIDEO MUSIC AWARDS. WE CREATED 16 INTERVIEW
SEGMENTS FROM AN IMAGINARY DOCUMENTARY IN WHICH
YOUNG ADULTS WERE ASKED QUESTIONS LOOSELY
BASED AROUND EACH AWARDS CATEGORY. OUR CONCEPT
WAS TO CAPTURE A 10-SECOND MOMENT IN THE CONTEXT
OF A LONGER DISCUSSION. SHOOTING IN A DOCUMEN-
TARY, LOW-BUDGET STYLE CREATED A REALISTIC VIEW OF
WHAT TODAY'S YOUTH ARE THINKING AND TALKING ABOUT.
THE TIGHT FRAMING OF THE SUBJECTS GIVES A SENSE OF
INTIMACY AS WELL AS FOCUSING THE ATTENTION ON THE
DIALOGUE. THE CASTING OF A DIVERSE AUDIENCE GAVE
US THE OPPORTUNITY TO PORTRAY MANY DIFFERENT
VIEWPOINTS ON LIFE AND THE INFLUENCE OF MUSIC.
TOPICS RANGED FROM CENSORSHIP TO MALE BALDNESS
TO THE INTERNET.

THE HENRY J. KAISER FAMILY FOUNDATION

It's Your (Sex) Life
Your Guide to Safe & Responsible Sex

fight for your rights:
protect yourself

PRINT/ IT'S YOUR (SEX) LIFE, 2000: EACH YEAR, THE CHANNEL FOCUSES ON AREAS OF IMPORTANCE TO YOUNG PEOPLE, FROM POLITICS TO AIDS AWARENESS, AND CREATES PROMOTIONAL CAMPAIGNS, REFERRED TO INTERNALLY AS "PRO-SOCIAL CAMPAIGNS," TO EDUCATE OUR AUDIENCE AND POINT THEM IN DIFFERENT DIRECTIONS TO LEARN MORE FOR THEMSELVES. THE FOCUS OF THE 2002 CAMPAIGN WAS SEXUAL HEALTH, AND OUR CHALLENGE WAS TO CREATE A PIECE THAT WOULD RESONATE WITH YOUNG PEOPLE AND ENCOURAGE THEM TO MAKE THIS A PRIORITY FOR THEMSELVES. TYPICALLY, SEXUAL HEALTH GUIDES ARE STRICT, CLINICAL PAMPHLETS LACKING VISUAL DYNAMISM. THEY DON'T TRY TO CONNECT WITH KIDS ON THEIR LEVEL. WE WANTED THE CONTENT TO CONFRONT THE SITUATIONS AND CONSEQUENCES THAT YOUNG PEOPLE ACTUALLY FACE ON A REGULAR BASIS, SO WE DECIDED TO USE REAL PEOPLE IN THEIR PERSONAL ENVIRONMENTS. WE HIRED DOCUMENTARY PHOTOGRAPHER, SCOTT HOUSTON, AND PUT TOGETHER A GROUP OF COUPLES TO GET IMAGES THAT ACCURATELY REFLECTED THE DIVERSITY AND REALITY OF OUR AUDIENCE. THERE WAS SOME INITIAL CONCERN FROM THE HIGHER-UPS THAT OUR IMAGES WOULD BE PERCEIVED AS TOO SUGGESTIVE, BUT THAT WAS EXACTLY WHAT WE WANTED: TO PROVOKE PEOPLE AND TO MAKE THEM THINK. SEX SELLS.

Introduction

How to Negotiate with Your Partner

Sexually Transmitted Diseases

Avoiding Unintended Pregnancy

How to Talk to Your Partner About Safer Sex

Whether you choose to have sex or not, it is important to be able to talk about sex. It can be uncomfortable to have direct conversations about sex, but it does get easier if you are confident about your facts. Bottom line: When it comes to sex, good communication is important, with friends, health care providers, parents/family, and your boyfriend or girlfriend.

If a couple is going to have sex, it's important for them to talk things over first. They need to discuss topics like their sexual boundaries and protection so they can protect themselves against pregnancy and STDs. It's important that couples ask each other about STDs. But remember, since others can't always be counted on to be honest about their STD status — especially because they may not even know they have one — using condoms for protection — always — is very important.

Of course, if you have an STD, it's good to be honest. Not only will it help you take the right precautions to protect your health and your partner's health — by either abstaining from sexual activity or using condoms and checking safer sex — it also shows your partner that you care for and respect him or her. Chances are, your partner will appreciate your truthfulness, and such honesty may even strengthen the emotional bond between you.

Here are some tips professionals offer about how to have that talk. Choose a time and place that's relaxed and comfortable before you get intimate (ideally, that means before you take your clothes off). Be sure to arm yourself with facts so that you can answer any questions your partner may have. You might want to start the conversation by asking your partner if he or she has ever been tested so that you really care for him or her and that's why you want to talk about STDs and protection. A part of what you want to tell your partner is about an STD you have, you might say that last year, you found out you carry HPV, or that you just learned that you have an STD, etc. If you have gential herpes, you might explain that you sometimes get sores in the genital area.

Keep it simple and just give the facts about symptoms, treatment, how the disease is spread, and how you can protect each other. This is a difficult conversation that will likely stir up a lot of emotions, but try to think of this as simply sharing vital information.

Then give your partner some time and space to digest the news. After all, it probably took you a while when you first heard. Offer to provide more information or an STD hotline number. With time, most people take the news pretty well and don't let it stand in the way of the relationship. Once the news is out, it's best to find out before the relationship goes too far. With everything that's been learned in recent years about STDs and their transmission, it's entirely possible for people with an STD to have a satisfying sex life without passing infection to their partners.

Getting Help

Finding a health care provider
The best person to talk to about health matters is a health care provider whom you trust. Finding that person can sometimes be difficult, but it doesn't necessarily have to be a doctor. Often, a nurse practitioner or nurse can help and may have more time to sit and answer questions.

If you want to find a reproductive health or women's health care clinic near you, look in the Yellow pages under "Birth Control Information Centers" or "Clinics" — specifically for those clinics that offer family planning services or STD testing services. You can also call your local Planned Parenthood office, or call the national Planned Parenthood hotline at 1-800-230-PLAN, and they will connect you to your nearest local provider. To find a clinic that provides tests and treatment for sexually transmitted diseases (STDs), look for the phone book for city or county health centers, or call the national hotline numbers listed on page 00.

In most cases, you're entitled to confidential treatment for STDs, pregnancy, and birth control no matter how old you are. To be sure, let your health care provider know if you want your visit — and anything discussed during it — to remain confidential. If you're under 18, you need to be aware that some states do have laws requiring parental notification or consent if you seek an abortion, although most states also allow a judge to make exceptions.

To find out the situation in your state, you can call your local Planned Parenthood office or the National Planned Parenthood hotline at 1-800-230-PLAN.

Of course, health care provides visits, STD tests, and contraception cost money, but if you have insurance Plans expenses can be covered, or at low cost and sometimes free confidential care is available at family planning clinics or STD clinics.

Talking with your family
Try talking with your parents or an adult you trust — maybe an older sibling, a teacher, a guidance counselor or an aunt or uncle. Even though it can be scary to raise certain issues, the rewards can be great. Family members know you better and can give you guidance based on the details of your personal situation. But if you need outside help as well, we've got some names and numbers to help you get started.

Other Resources
To find out more about your sexual health, to keep up on what's going on in the fight For Your Rights campaign, or to get involved locally, log on to: www.fightforyourrights.info.com.

the perks of being a wallflower

stephen chbosky

Thin Skin

emma forrest
author of Namedropper

"A truly remarkable, hilarious, and devastating work of fiction."
—Jerry Stahl, author of Permanent Midnight

brave

NEW GIRL   Louisa Luna

meg castaldo   the foreigner /

PRINT/ MTV FICTION BOOK LINE, 1999-2003: LET'S FACE IT...WE ALL JUDGE A BOOK BY ITS COVER. IT'S THE REASON WE PICK IT UP IN THE FIRST PLACE. WORKING ON MTV FICTION FOR THE PAST FEW YEARS HAS BEEN ESPECIALLY REWARDING BECAUSE IT'S ABOUT CREATING A VISUAL TRANSLATION OF THE PRINTED WORD. IT HAS INVOLVED COLLABORATING WITH TALENTED YOUNG PHOTOGRAPHERS AND DESIGNERS, FEEDING OFF EACH OTHER'S IMAGINATIONS, AND USING BOLD COLOR COMBINA-TIONS, IRREVERENT IMAGES AND FRESH TYPOGRAPHY. COLLECTED TOGETHER, THE COVERS FORM A SERIES OF SEXY, MINI, URBAN FASHION POSTERS.

ON-AIR DESIGN/ SO CAL SUMMER, 2000:
MTV'S SUMMER BEACH HOUSE FOR
2000 WAS LOCATED ON THE BOARDWALK
IN PACIFIC BEACH, IN SAN DIEGO. WE
WANTED TO CAPTURE THE DISTINCT
LIFESTYLE OF SOUTHERN CALIFORNIA
YOUTH CULTURE AS WELL AS EMBRACE
THE LOCAL BEAUTY OF THE AREA ITSELF.
SCENARIOS INCLUDED WERE: A DRIVE
DOWN THE PACIFIC COAST HIGHWAY, A
RIDE ON A ROLLER COASTER, A GROUP
OF KIDS SKATEBOARDING DOWN THE
BOARDWALK, SURFERS PULLING UP TO
THE PARKING LOT WITH THEIR BOARDS,
A ROLLERSKATER WITH HEAPHONES
ON GROOVING TO THE MUSIC, AND A
SUNSET JAM SESSION ON THE BEACH
BY A FIRE.

INTERNATIONAL ON-AIR PROMO/ KEBAB,
2000: THIS PROMO WAS ONE OF 15 IMAGE
SPOTS CREATED TO PROMOTE A LATE-
NIGHT PROGRAMMING ZONE ON MTV
UK. THE STORY IS OF TWO BROTHERS
WHO ARE KEBAB SHOP OWNERS WHO
SERVE LATE-NIGHT FOOD ONLY TO
RETIRE TO A BACK ROOM TO WRESTLE
IN FULL OLYMPIC STYLE WHEN BUSINESS
IS SLOW. HERE, TENSION IS MOUNTING
AS BROTHER ONE SINGS ALONG,
KARAOKE-STYLE, TO THE BRITNEY
SPEARS TRACK "...BABY ONE MORE TIME"
IN A FLAGRANT ATTEMPT TO WIND UP
BROTHER TWO AND START A SCRAP.
NO DOUBT IT WILL END IN A WRESTLE.

ON-AIR PROMO/ VIDEOS WORK HERE, 2001: IN THIS PROMO, VIDEOS ARE PERSONIFIED, SOMEWHAT POETICALLY, AS WORKING STIFFS. THEY APPEAR ON THE AIR, PERFORM FOR A FEW MINUTES, THEN RETURN TO THE RACK TO WAIT UNTIL THEY'RE NEEDED AGAIN, DAY AFTER DAY, UNTIL THEY'RE NO LONGER CALLED UPON. WE WANTED TO ILLUSTRATE WHAT VIDEOS DO WHEN THEY'RE NOT ON THE AIR. HERE, THEY ARE CELEBRATING THE RETIREMENT FROM THE *TRL* COUNTDOWN OF ONE OF THEIR OWN. THE PARTY IS COMPLETE WITH CAMEOS BY VETERANS FROM MTV'S EARLY DAYS COMMENTING RUEFULLY ON THE MODERN VIDEO WORLD. THE PIECE ENDS SADLY WITH A VIDEO CALLING *TRL* TO VOTE FOR ITSELF, SOMETHING WE IMAGINED TO BE THE LEAST COOL THING A VIDEO COULD DO.

AUDIO:

I WANNA BE BAD: "C'mon everyone! 'More Than That''s being retired today!"

U REMIND ME: "I love retirement day."
WHEN IT'S OVER: "How come?"
U REMIND ME: "Frees up a spot in the countdown."
WHEN IT'S OVER: [Nods thoughtfully] "Hmmm."

MORE THAN THAT: "Thanks, guys. And thanks to you old videos who came back for my big day."

SEPARATE WAYS: "These videos got it easy—remember, we'd go on 60, 70 times a day…"
YOU BETTER RUN: "Well, there was so few of us then…"
SUPER FREAK: "And special effects? We got dry ice and we liked it."
SEPARATE WAYS: "Eh, videos today… they all think they're movies."

PA: "'More Than That,' you're on."

WHEN IT'S OVER [Whispering]: "Uh, yeah, I'd like to vote for 'When It's Over'…"

CHYRON:

MTV. Videos work here.

PRINT/ *LIFE IS SWEET* – 1998 VIDEO MUSIC AWARDS BOOK: THE IDEA HERE WAS TO EXPLORE THE SIDE OF MUSIC THAT DOES NOT MAKE IT TO MTV: THE EVERYDAY LOVE, EXPRESSION AND COMMITMENT TO THE ART AND DIVERSITY OF MAKING MUSIC THAT THRIVES, REGARDLESS OF FAME AND FORTUNE. SO IN THE SPOTLIGHT OF THE VIDEO MUSIC AWARDS, WE HONORED BUT A FEW OF THE MANY UNSUNG HEROES. WE SENT PHOTOGRAPHER MICHAEL MCGLAULIN ON A ROAD TRIP ACROSS THE COUNTRY AND A WRITER FOLLOWED UP VIA PHONE TO GET SOME GREAT QUOTES. WITH MICHAEL AND A RESEARCH TEAM LOOKING FOR LEADS, IT WAS OFTEN STRESSFUL HOPING WE WOULD COME UP WITH ENOUGH GOOD STUFF; HOWEVER, THE SHEER EXCITEMENT AND JOY OF FINDING THESE PEOPLE KEPT EVERYTHING GOING.

People like to bang on stuff.

NICK: Being able to write is exhilarating in the aspect that I get to let out some of the things that I've learned. Then when I get to entertain, I get to bring people together in one place at one time, and I think that's a good thing.

I thought it would be cool to make a go at supporting myself as a musician, and I actually got a record deal, but I didn't do that much music 'cause there was so much other BS that went along with it. All I wanted to do was go out and play, and we couldn't because our record was on hold. It ended up breaking my heart, because this is the thing that I had every thumb in the pie for. I put this together; I had to watch it die. There was about two months after Horse broke up where I just didn't want to touch a guitar. 'Cause it was a lot my decision to call it a day. Then one day, Chuck, my buddy that plays drums, invited me to jam in his basement. He calls his friend Ron, a bassist. So Ron comes over, and we're all of a like mind, all no bullshit dudes, and all we want to do is play. After our first jam, we just sat there listeningto the tape that we made. Chuck is thirty seven, Ron is thirty four, I'm twenty six—I said, "Dude, when was the last time you guys sat around after practice and listened to the tape that you recorded on the boom box and got stoked? It's been, like, since eighth grade!" It was cool just to have that again. I was like, "If we never get out of the basement, I don't ever really give a shit." That's when I really started to get into it again. I was smiling again.

BANJO: ...for shit and giggles...

ON-AIR PROMO/   THE WAYANS BROTHERS, 2000: MTV'S 2000 VIDEO MUSIC AWARDS SHOW WAS HOSTED BY THE WAYANS BROTHERS. SHAWN + MARLON WAYANS WERE REALLY HOT AT THE TIME BECAUSE OF THEIR BOX OFFICE SMASH HIT *SCARY MOVIE*. WE WENT TO THEIR HOUSE TO DISCUSS IDEAS. THE BOYS SUGGESTED MANY WILD CONCEPTS. IN THE END, WE DECIDED THAT THE WAYANS BROTHERS DRESSED UP AS THE WILLIAMS SISTERS WOULD BE HYSTERICAL AND THAT THEIR BROTHER KEENAN SHOULD PLAY MR. WILLIAMS, THE GIRLS' FATHER. WE GOT EXACT REPLICAS OF THEIR OUTFITS MADE, INCLUDING, MOST IMPORTANT, THEIR BEADS AND BRAIDS. WE ALSO THOUGHT IT WOULD BE FUNNY TO HAVE MR. WILLIAMS HOLD UP CUE CARDS AS HE HAD RECENTLY DONE AT WIMBLEDON. WE SCOUTED A PRIVATE TENNIS COURT NEAR AARON SPELLING'S HOME IN L.A., RENOVATED THE GROUNDS, AND LET THE BOYS HAVE FUN.

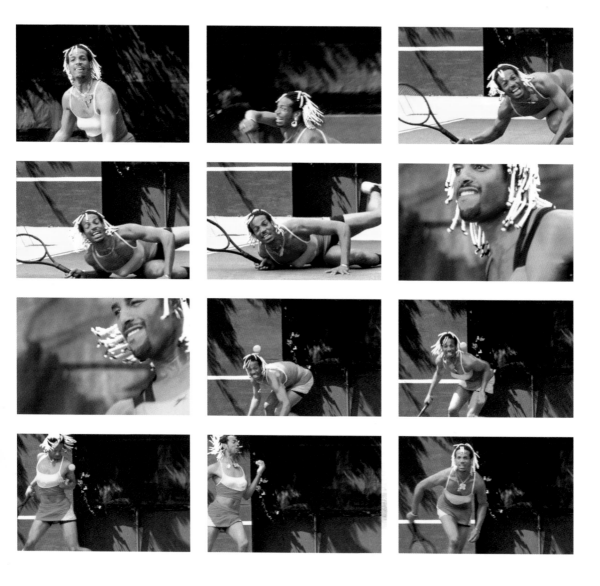

INTERNATIONAL ON-AIR PROMO/   COORDINATES, 2002: THIS WAS MTV'S FIRST INTERNATIONALLY COPRODUCED CAMPAIGN. CELEBRATING THE DIVERSE PERSPECTIVES OF PEOPLE AROUND THE WORLD, THE CAMPAIGN FEATURED A SERIES OF 21 SPOTS, EACH HIGHLIGHTING KEY WORDS CHOSEN BY THE INDIVIDUAL CHANNELS, SUCH AS *RHYTHM*, *COMMUNITY*, *IDENTITY*, *SEX*, *CHAOS*, *LAUGHTER*, AND *BEAUTY*. EACH WORD WAS INTERPRETED BY A SERIES OF ORIGINAL IMAGES TAKEN ALL OVER THE WORLD BY PHOTOGRAPHERS COMMISSIONED LOCALLY BY EACH OF THE DIRECTOR/PRODUCERS. SET TO VIBRANT AND ECLECTIC SOUNDTRACKS, THE 30-SECOND SPOTS WERE LINKED TOGETHER BY GRAPHICS CONCEPTUALIZED BY FERNANDO LAZZARI OF MTV LATIN AMERICA AND FEATURED THE EXACT LATITUDE AND LONGITUDE COORDINATES REPRESENTED IN EACH OF THE STILLS.   EVERYONE AGREED TO SHOOT 35-MILLIMETER SLIDES, AND EACH DIRECTOR WAS GIVEN COMPLETE CREATIVE CONTROL OF HIS OR HER SPOT (IMAGE SELECTION, EDITORIAL STYLE AND SOUND DESIGN.) EACH PARTICIPATING MTV CHANNEL PRODUCED ONE PROMO, BUT ALL CHANNELS SHOWED THE ENTIRE SERIES OF SPOTS ON-AIR. MTV CHANNELS AND WEB SITES PARTICIPATING IN MTV COORDINATES INCLUDED AUSTRALIA, BRAZIL, CANADA, SPAIN, EUROPE, FRANCE, GERMANY, INDIA, ITALY, JAPAN, KOREA, LATIN AMERICA, MANDARIN, NETHERLANDS, NORDIC, POLAND, RUSSIA, SOUTHEAST ASIA, THE U.K., AND THE U.S.   THE IMAGES THAT FOLLOW ARE: *SLEEP*, *BEAUTY*, *FOOTBALL*, *SEX*, *HOME*.

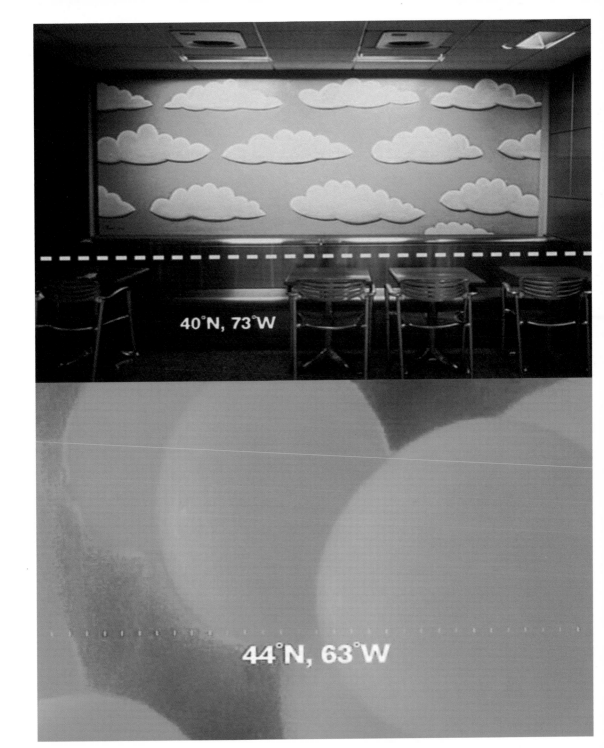

40°N, 73°W

51°N, 114°W

48°N, 2°E

23°S, 46°W

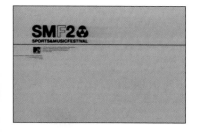

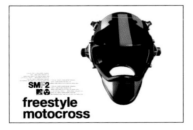

ON-AIR DESIGN/ SPORTS & MUSIC FESTIVAL 2, 1998: THE SPORTS AND MUSIC FESTIVAL IS A HYBRID OF ATHLETIC COMPETITIONS AND MUSICAL PERFORMANCES. WE BUILT ON THE IDEA OF THIS THEME BY IMAGINING A RESEARCH-AND-DEVELOPMENT FACILITY THAT PRODUCES HYBRID, MUTANT MACHINES—SPORTS EQUIPMENT CROSSBRED WITH AUDIO GEAR. WE KNEW WHAT THE GRAPHICS WERE FOR ON-AIR DESIGN, ADVERTISING, POSTERS, SHOW SETS, EVEN CLOTHING AND PRODUCT. IN RESPONSE TO THESE, WE WANTED TO COME UP WITH A DESIGN THAT WAS MORE OF AN OVERALL IDENTITY SYSTEM THAN A SINGLE LOGO AND LOOK. WE BUILT AN ENTIRE VISUAL VOCABULARY OF ELEMENTS THAT COULD BE RECOMBINED AS NECESSARY.

ON-AIR DESIGN/ 1999 FASHIONABLY LOUD MIAMI: THE CONCEPT WAS TO CAPTURE THE ESSENCE OF A HIGH-END FASHION SHOOT AND COMBINE THAT WITH AN ABSTRACT AUDIO TRACK. WE LOOKED AT OBSCURE FASHION MAGAZINES AND RESPONDED TO THE CLINICAL LOOK OF FASHION PHOTOGRAPHY. WE SET UP A TRADITIONAL FASHION SHOOT WITH A FASHION PHOTOGRAPHER AND HAIR AND MAKEUP PEOPLE. ORIGINALLY, WE WERE PLANNING TO SCAN IN THOUSANDS OF PRINTS CHOSEN FROM THE SHOOT SO THAT WE COULD GET THE DEFINITION AND QUALITY OF A FASHION SPREAD IN A MAGAZINE, BUT AT THE SUGGESTION OF THE PHOTOGRAPHER, WE WERE ABLE TO SAVE HUGE AMOUNTS OF TIME AND LABOR BY USING NEW DIGITAL EQUIPMENT. WE USED A DIGITAL ATTACHMENT ON THE CAMERA AND A PROGRAM FOR DOWNLOADING EVERY IMAGE. EACH IMAGE WAS THEN INTERPRETED AS A SINGLE FRAME WHEN IT CAME TIME TO EDIT. AN ELECTRONIC DEVICE WAS BUILT TO EXECUTE A SMOOTH 360-DEGREE TURN OF THE CHAIRS THAT THE MODELS SAT ON, ENABLING US TO BLEND THE DIFFERENT MODELS SEAMLESSLY. A WIND MACHINE CREATED ADDITIONAL MOTION.   AMBER MUSIC WAS COMMISSIONED TO CREATE ORIGINAL SOUND WITH AN ETHEREAL, ABSTRACT QUALITY.

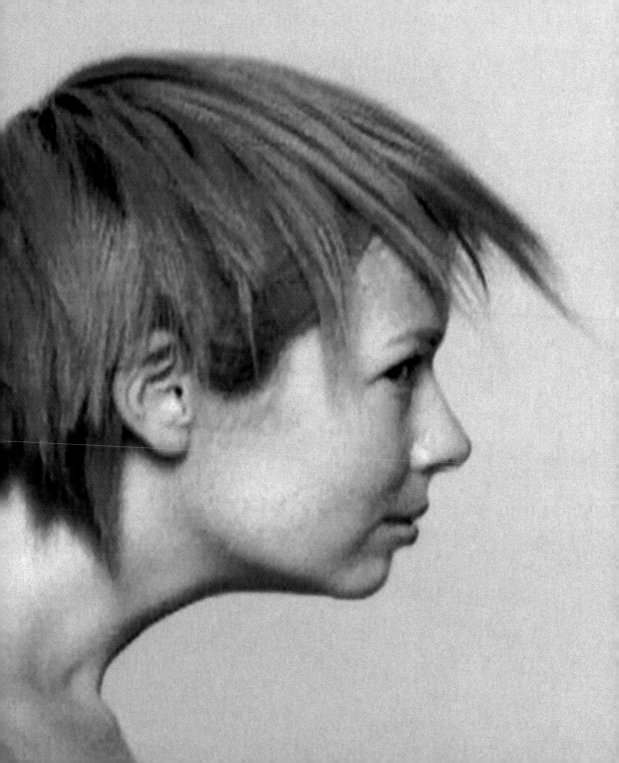

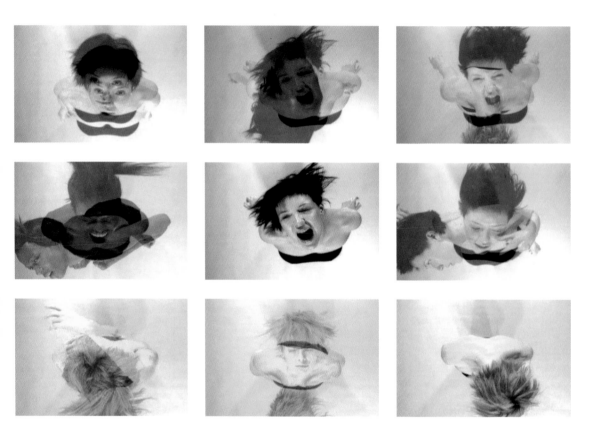

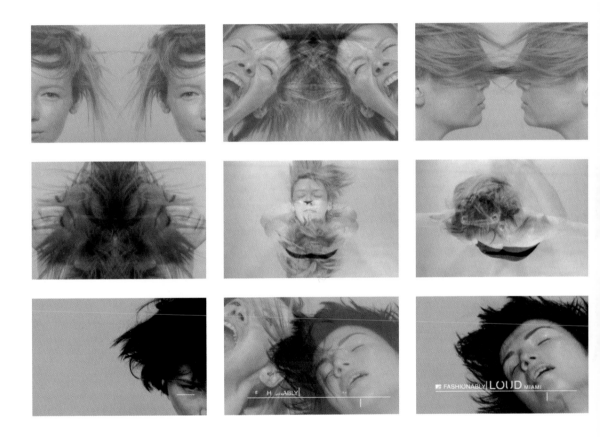

ON-AIR PROMO/ TENACIOUS D OSBOURNES, 2002: WHEN I WAS YOUNG, MY PARENTS WARNED ME TIME AND TIME AGAIN: "RODMAN, NEVER PLAY WITH BLACK MAGIC," AND ALL I CAN SAY NOW IS: I'M REALLY SORRY, MOM AND DAD. YES, IT'S TRUE, I SOLD MY SOUL TO MAKE THIS PROMO, AND I'M ASHAMED TO SAY THAT IF I COULD DO IT ALL OVER, I'D DEFINITELY DO IT AGAIN! JACK BLACK AND KYLE GASS WERE AMAZING TO WORK WITH, AND IT'S MY BELIEF THAT THEY MAY HAVE "CROSSED OVER" THAT DAY, BECAUSE THEY SEEMED TO BE POSSESSED BY WHAT I CAN ONLY DESCRIBE AS AN OTHERWORLDLY POWER. BUT I GUESS THAT'S WHAT IT TAKES TO DELIVER THE SINGLE GREATEST HOMAGE TO OZZY THAT THIS WORLD'S EVER SEEN. VIVA TENACIOUS D!

AUDIO:
"The Osbournes, the family that came straight out of hell.
Ozzy is the daddy and he's ringing the bell.
Jack is the son and he's gotta big brain and he's gotta big fro on his head.
Kelly is the daughter and she couldn't be no harder. Oh, she's sassy and she's made outta lead.
Sharon's Ozzy's wife and she saved his crazy life. She's bustin' Ozzy's balls and she's tearin' down the halls.
The Osbourne family show.
The Osbourne family show."

ON-AIR PROMO/ NUMBER-ONE FRIEND, 2002: NUMBER-ONE FRIEND IS REALLY THE NUMBER-ONE FRIEND TO EVERYONE. FOR A LITTLE YELLOW GUY, HE'S GOT A LOT OF HEART AND A BIG BONER FOR MUSIC. I FIRST MET NUMBER-ONE FRIEND WHEN I WAS VISITING THE BLUE LAGOON HOT SPRINGS JUST OUTSIDE OF REYKJAVÍK, ICELAND. HE WAS THERE ON TOUR WITH CIRQUE D' SOLEIL. IT TURNED OUT HIS GIRLFRIEND KNEW MINE FROM CHEERLEADING CAMP, AND SHE INTRODUCED US. WE HIT IT OFF RIGHT AWAY. I CONVINCED HIM TO COME TO NEW YORK CITY AND SHOOT SOME SPOTS FOR MTV2. ALTHOUGH HE IS NOT YOUR TYPICAL LEADING-MAN TYPE, HIS PERSONALITY AND LOVE OF MUSIC MADE HIM PERFECT FOR THE CHANNEL. COINCIDENTALLY, BUSTA RHYMES WAS IN NEW YORK CITY RECORDING HIS NEW ALBUM, SO I FLEW NUMBER ONE FRIEND IN AND SET HIM UP OVER AT THE DAYS INN, IN JERSEY, TO SAVE MONEY. BUSTA SHOWED UP FIVE HOURS LATE FOR THE SHOOT, BUT NUMBER-ONE FRIEND WAS COMPLETELY PROFESSIONAL ABOUT IT. WE JUST SAT AROUND TALKING SHOP WHILE WE WAITED, DISCUSSING HAMS AND STUFF. AND THAT'S HOW THE WHOLE HAM IDEA CAME TOGETHER, RIGHT THERE ON THE DAY OF THE SHOOT.

AUDIO: "This is Busta Rhymes. Flipmode is the squad! And when you watch MTV2, you get videos all day, every day, all music around the clock. So in the meantime, what you need to do is throw your hands in the air, ain't playin' with y'all."

PRINT/ *FETISH* – 1997 VIDEO MUSIC AWARDS BOOK: STACY AND I USED TO DRIVE TOGETHER ON A VERY LONG COMMUTE TO NEW YORK CITY EVERY DAY. THE CAR RIDE PROVIDED A MOVING SANCTUARY IN WHICH MUCH DEBATE, DISCUSSION, AND BRAINSTORMING HAPPENED ON DESIGN IN GENERAL AND, MORE SPECIFICALLY, THE VMA BOOKS. YOU START WITH SEEDS, WHICH BECOME SPROUTS, WHICH GROW INTO PLANTS. HOW COOL WOULD A RUBBER COVER BE? BUT WHAT WOULD THAT MEAN? THIS LED US TO ASSOCIATE IT WITH FETISHES. THE DEFINITION OF THE WORD *FETISH* HAD BEEN HIJACKED FROM BEING SIMPLY A TALISMAN TO EMBODYING A MORE KINKY SEXUAL EXPERIENCE AND THAT IS CERTAINLY WHAT THE COVER ALLUDED TO. THEN THERE IS THE NOTION OF THINKING BIG AND JUST SAYING, WHY NOT? CAN WE ACTUALLY GET FAMOUS FOLKS FROM THE ARTS AND ENTERTAINMENT, ARCHITECTURE, FASHION, AND POLITICAL WORLDS TO LET US HOLD AND PHOTOGRAPH THE VERY THING THAT THEY CHERISH MOST? IT WAS A SLOW START, BUT IT GOT BETTER WHEN WE HAD A FEW CONFIRMATIONS, AS ALMOST EVERYONE WANTED TO KNOW WHO ELSE WAS IN THE BOOK. BY THE END, WE HAD TO TURN PEOPLE AWAY. A DEADLINE IS A DEADLINE.

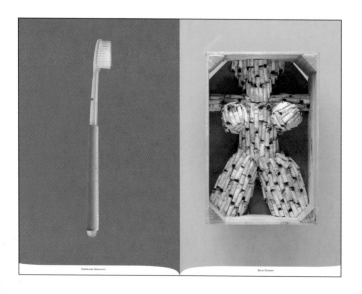

STEPHANIE SEYMOUR   BECK HANSEN

MICHAEL STIPE

CHEMICAL BROTHERS   ANTON CORBIN

DEAN KARR

ON-AIR DESIGN/ TIMES SQUARE PACKAGING, 2000: "TIMES SQUARE IS MTV'S PLAYGROUND" WAS THE THEME FOR MTV'S LAUNCH INTO THE YEAR 2000. WE WANTED TO TAKE A FRESH LOOK AT OUR LOCATION IN TIMES SQUARE AND ILLUSTRATE THE INTERACTION BETWEEN THE STUDIO AND THE ENVIRONMENT OUTSIDE. THIS SERIES OF SPOTS FEATURED OUR MTV ASPIRATIONAL AUDIENCE FLOATING ABOVE TRAFFIC, BREAK DANCING ON THE SIDE OF MILITARY ISLAND, RISING ABOVE THE CROWDS TO WAVE INTO THE WINDOWS AND DANCING IN THE SUBWAY.   THE TIMES SQUARE BACKGROUND PLATES WERE SHOT FIRST. THEN THE PEOPLE WERE SHOT SEPARATELY ON BLUE SCREEN. ALL OF THE ROUGH CUTS WERE DONE ON AN AVID, THEN THE FINAL KEY WAS COMPLETED IN THE FLAME. ALL OF THE GRAPHICS WERE BASED AROUND ANIMATING OUT FROM ONE SINGLE CUBE.

ON-AIR PROMO/ JANET JACKSON ICON, 2001: COLOR TV. JANET JACKSON IS VERY MUCH A PRODUCT OF THE MTV GENERATION—HER DANCE STYLE, HER MUSIC, HER SEXUALITY. *MTV:ICON* WAS ALL ABOUT HONORING HER SINGULAR PLACE IN THE MTV ERA. TO ILLUSTRATE THAT, WE IMAGINED HOW SHE MIGHT HAVE GONE OVER DURING OTHER TIME PERIODS—THE 40'S, THE 50'S AND THE 60'S. THE ANSWER? NOT VERY WELL. HERE, A 1950'S SITCOM FAMILY'S FIRST COLOR TV EXPERIENCE IS NOT WHAT THEY EXPECTED WHEN A SEXY, STRANGE JANET VIDEO IS THE FIRST THING THEY SEE. IF THIS IS WHAT YOU GET WITH A COLOR TV, THEN THEY WANT NO PART OF IT.

AUDIO:
DAD: "I've got it, everyone, I've got it! Our first color TV!"
MOM: "C'mon kids, it's here!"
KIDS: "Yay!!!"
DAD: "Oh, this is going to be great! "
KIDS: "Turn it on! Turn it on!"
DAD: "All right, everyone. here goes!"

[The family sits in stunned silence.]

CHYRON:
The world wasn't always ready for Janet.

We are.
MTV: Icon / Janet Jackson

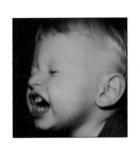

PRINT/ *9999* – 1999 VIDEO MUSIC AWARDS BOOK: WE WANTED TO TIE THE BOOK INTO THE END OF THE CENTURY AND WERE VERY MUCH INSPIRED BY THE AIR DATE OF THE SHOW, 9.9.99, SO WE THOUGHT ABOUT THE THINGS THAT SINK IN, THE THINGS THAT SIMPLY ARE, THE SIGHTS, THOUGHTS, WORDS, COLORS AND FEELINGS THAT INSPIRE SONGS. I NEVER COUNTED, BUT THERE ARE MOST LIKELY 10,000 INSPIRATIONS IN THIS BOOK, FROM FAMILY PHOTOS TO 306 NAMES FOR GOD (THERE ARE NUMEROUS REFERENCES TO THE NUMBER NINE THROUGHOUT), FROM 504 PLACES TO OUTSTANDING PHOTOS FROM A SELECT GROUP OF FRIENDS. TO TOP IT OFF, WE DID NINE DIFFERENT COVERS. WHILE THE DESIGNER WAS PUTTING THE PHOTOS TOGETH-ER, SOMETHING POWERFUL BEGAN TO EMERGE. STRINGS OF PHOTOS TURNED THEMSELVES INTO DIFFERENT VISUAL SONGS WHILE PERSONAL AND AUTOBIOGRAPHICAL NARRATIVES GRACEFULLY EMERGED AND TOOK FORM. IT IS CERTAINLY THE MOST INTIMATE AND REFLECTIVE BOOK WE HAVE DONE, A SIMULTANEOUS LOOK BACK AND LOOK FORWARD TO THE NEW MILLENNI-UM.

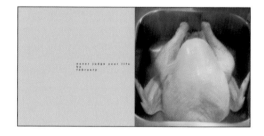

ON-AIR PROMO/ PRODIGY + CHRIS ROCK, 1997: WE WERE ASSIGNED TO THE PROMOTION OF THE 1997 VIDEO MUSIC AWARDS KNOWING ONLY THE FOLLOWING AS WE BEGAN THE PROJECT: CHRIS ROCK IS HOSTING. MUSIC VIDEOS NEED TO BE THE FOCUS. OUR HOST IS A COMEDIAN, SO THE PROMOS BETTER BE FUNNY. WE THOUGHT IT WOULD BE FUN TO PUT CHRIS INTO VISUALLY STUNNING, AND HIGH-ENERGY PERFORMANCE MUSIC VIDEOS THAT WERE UP FOR AWARDS THAT YEAR. WE RAN THROUGH LOADS OF VIDEOS UNTIL IT WAS NARROWED DOWN TO THE FOLLOWING THREE: JAMIROQUAI'S "VIRTUAL INSANITY," WILL SMITH'S "MEN IN BLACK" AND PRODIGY'S "BREATHE." EACH OF THE VIDEOS CAME WITH UNIQUE WARDROBE AND PERFORMANCE REQUIREMENTS. IN THE PRODIGY VIDEO, CHRIS NEEDED TO BE TOPLESS. THE BAND MEMBER HE WAS REPLACING HAD NO SHIRT ON, LOTS OF PIERCINGS, AND A BUNCH OF TATTOOS. WELL, IF WE WANTED TO KEEP IT AUTHENTIC, HE NEEDED ALL OF THE ABOVE TO COME TO LIFE. CHRIS ROCK PLAYED ALONG. THIS SPOT WAS ALSO THE FIRST PROJECT I EVER WORKED ON IN WHICH WE GOT TO FILM SCRIPTED LINES SUCH AS, "HEY, YOU! SHUT THE FUCK UP IN THERE! I'M TRYING TO TELL THESE PEOPLE ABOUT THE MTV VIDEO MUSIC AWARDS!"

PRINT/ 1999 VIDEO MUSIC AWARDS PRINT CAMPAIGN: WHO WOULD HAVE IMAGINED MTV AT THE FAMOUS METROPOLITAN OPERA HOUSE? SO WHY NOT CAST MUSICAL ARTISTS IN CLASSIC OPERA ROLES FOR A PRINT CAMPAIGN TO PROMOTE THE SHOW? ALL THE ARTISTS HAD A BLAST AND WERE VERY MUCH IN THE SPIRIT OF THE ROLES THEY WERE POR-TRAYING. IN A FUNNY WAY, THE ROLES KIND OF MATCHED UP WELL WITH THEIR PERSONALITIES; INTENTIONAL OR SUBLIMINAL IS YOUR GUESS. SOME THINGS ARE BEST KEPT SECRET.

ON-AIR PROMO/ THE JUKKA BROS., 1999: THE SUN BARELY SHONE THROUGH THE MIST AND OVER THE KNEES OF BIG JUKKA ULF, A DIRECTOR AT TRAKTOR. HIS BUTT HAD BEEN CHOSEN AS THE MOST PHOTOGENIC, AS LITTLE JUKKA'S ACTUAL BEHIND WAS A TAD HAIRY. OH, HOW WE SLAPPED HIM. HE STILL HAS THE MTV LOGO ON HIS BUTT, BUT NOW HE IS A LOT HAIRIER AND YOU CANNOT REALLY SEE IT ANYMORE. UNLESS YOU ARE A GOOD FRIEND OF ULF'S. PAUL & LINUS FROM FALLON MCELLIGOT, A NEW YORK AD AGENCY, WERE GIVEN A BRIEF TO DRAMATIZE THE WAY IN WHICH MTV REACHES EVERY LITTLE NOOK AND CRANNY OF THE WORLD WITH ITS CULTURAL INFLUENCE AND SEXY PROGRAMMING. THEY INVENTED THE FOUR BROTHERS WHO LIVE SOMEWHERE "FAR FAR AWAY FROM NEW YORK, CHICAGO, AND L.A." THEN THEY CAME TO US WITH THE SCRIPTS. WE BUILT THE BIG HOUSE AND THE LITTLE HOUSE IN THE WOODS OUTSIDE OF STOCKHOLM, SWEDEN. WE CAST LARGELY FINNISH ACTORS FOR THE BROTHERS. THE YOUNGEST, LITTLE JUKKA, HOWEVER, IS A SWEDISH TRUCK DRIVER WHOM WE HAVE LEARNED TO CHERISH OVER THE YEARS. HE GETS SPANKED. THE HOUSES WORKED FOR BOTH INTERIORS AND EXTERIORS, SO WE COULD LITERALLY GO MAD IN THE COUNTRY. THE SHOOT WAS LONG AND HIGHLY ENTERTAINING. WE THINK IT WAS REASONABLY SUCCESSFUL. THE JUKKA BROS. HANDED OUT THE AWARD FOR BEST ALBUM AT THE EUROPEAN MTV AWARDS THAT YEAR, AND VANITY FAIR FEATURED THEM OVER TWO PAGES (SHOT BY DAVID LACHAPELLE) IN THEIR 1999 "HALL OF FAME." WE WANTED TO DO A MOVIE, BUT HAD LOST THEIR PHONE NUMBERS BY THEN. JUKKA BROS., IF YOU ARE READING THIS, PLEASE CALL.

INTERNATIONAL ON-AIR PROMO JAPAN/ SUSHI CHEF, 2000:
THE IDEA ORIGINATED WITH MY OBSERVATION THAT
EVERYDAY LIFE IN JAPAN IS DRIVEN BY STRESS. I CREATED
A CHARACTER, A TYPICAL "SALARYMAN" WHO FIGHTS
BACK AND DESTROYS THIS STRESS WITH ORIGINALITY
AND A SENSE OF HUMOR IN A SHORT-STORY FORMAT.

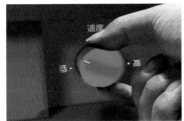

PRINT/ *WORSHIP* – 2002 VIDEO MUSIC AWARDS BOOK: THE THEME FOR THE 2002 VMA'S WAS WORSHIP. WE WANTED TO EXPLORE THE UNIQUE RELATIONSHIP SOME FANS HAVE WITH THE CELEBRITIES THEY ADMIRE AND PERHAPS EVEN WORSHIP. WE HIRED PHOTOGRAPHER DEWEY NICKS TO TRAVEL ACROSS THE COUNTRY AND FIND THE ULTIMATE FANS AND TRIBUTE ARTISTS TO SHOW HOW SOME PEOPLE CAN BLUR THE LINES BETWEEN FAME AND FANATACISM.

 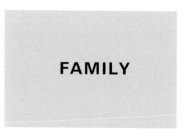 

INTERNATIONAL ON-AIR PROMO EUROPE,
2000: ANTON CORBIJN LED THE CRE-
ATIVE FOR THIS MTV EUROPE PROMO
FEATURING DAVE GROHL.

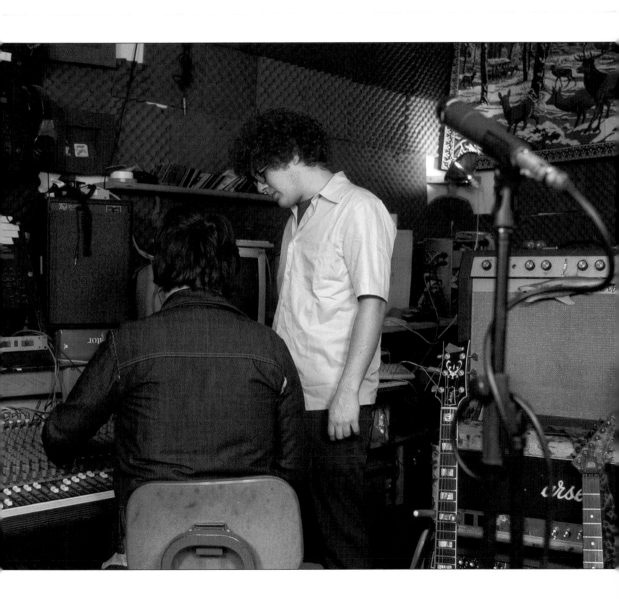

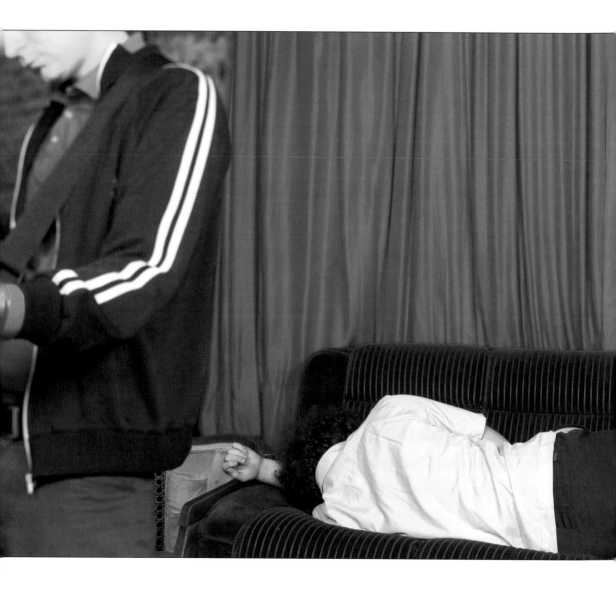

NOT TEFLON CREDITS

EDITED BY
Jeffrey Keyton

COMPILED BY
Jeffrey Keyton, Christina Norman + Kevin MacKall

ART DIRECTION + DESIGN
Stacy Drummond

TEXT EDITOR
Jacob Hoye

PROJECT MANAGEMENT
Sarah James

GRAPHIC ART SUPERVISION
Patti Rogoff + Danielle King

GRAPHIC ART
Michael Skinner

CLEARANCE
Andrea Glanz + Michelle Gurney

SPECIAL THANKS
Chie Arakai, Thomas Berger, Richard Browd, Hillary Cohen, Mike Densmore, Eileen Doherty, Walter Einenkel, Heidi Eskenazi, Tina Exharos, David Felton, Kathleen Jayes, Elinor Johnston, Morgan Korn, David Laidler, Estelle Leeds, Jamie Manalio, Jen Mandell, Romy Mann, Judy McGrath, Charles Miers, Susannah Nilosek, Fon-Lin Nyeu, Eva Prinz, Jerri Rose, Lance Rusoff, Melissa Sandoval, Lisa Silfen, Donald Silvey, Pam Sommers, Micah Sperling, Van Toffler, Chrsitopher Truch, Marci Villanueva, Billy Zimmer

EXTRA SPECIAL THANKS
Jim Debarros, David Horowitz, Danielle King, Paul Raphaelson, Wayne Rosenbaum , Christopher Thom + Oleg Troyanovsky

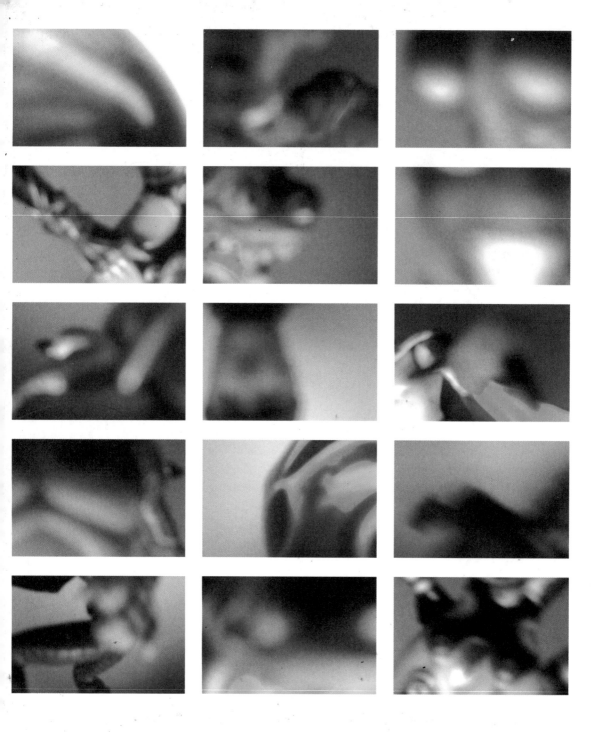